Find It, Fix It, Flip It

How to MAKE REAL MONEY in Real Estate Investing ONE HOUSE AT A TIME

Find It, Fix It, Flip It

How to MAKE REAL MONEY in Real Estate Investing ONE HOUSE AT A TIME

A Grassroots Guide to Real Estate Investing

By

Scott H. Williams

ISBN: 979-8-67404-525-0

Contents

Introduction

MY PASSION FOR real estate began in 1991 when my family sold the house that we grew up in, in Atlanta, Georgia. I was the youngest of three sons and a graduating senior at Morehouse College. This was a major crossroads and launching point for my family members, as everyone went their separate ways upon the selling of our house. Not only was I intrigued by the transaction process, but I was also instrumental in helping my mom locate a buyer and making sure the property was in sellable condition. That transaction always stood with me, even after I graduated from college with a BA degree in marketing and attempted to start a career in corporate America.

As the years went by, I quickly realized that I did not have the aptitude or the desire to work a traditional nine-to-five gig in corporate America. Even though my college experience trained me and I was well groomed to do so, I learned early on that my path would be one that marches to the beat of a different drum.

Therefore, in 1996, just before the start of the Olympics in Atlanta, Georgia, I took a leap of faith and left my job in marketing and invested all of the little monies that I had to start a real estate investment and mortgage company outfit in downtown Atlanta. I had been previously introduced to a gentleman who was a loan officer for a mortgage company; he was looking to start his own mortgage company. I, of course, was interested in branching out on my own for the first time, so we came together in partnership to invest in real estate and to provide mortgage loans in the metro Atlanta area. He would head up the mortgage company side, and I would head up the real estate investment side. We sublet an office from a larger company in midtown, and thus began my quest for knowledge in the real estate game.

I was like a sponge: I read every book on investing that I could get my hands on; I became a member of the Georgia Real Estate Investors Association; I went to seminars and networking events and even attended the last live presentation by Carlton Sheets in Tampa, Florida, who was at that point the king of real estate investing. I met with hard money lenders, and of course they were eager to provide funding at a 15 percent interest rate and five points in fees on the deal, paid up front at closing. I met with wholesalers who were eager to sell distressed properties for a $2,500 nonrefundable earnest money check; there were contractors promising the world on how they could rehab the properties on time and on budget. Then there were the attorneys and the accountants who could set up a limited liability company (LLC) to purchase and sell the properties and to take advantage of any write-offs and legal loopholes to save on capital gains.

I was on information overload. It was so much to take in during such a short period of time because we were on the clock now. We had bills to pay, rent that was due, and employees on both the mortgage side and the real estate investing side.

Then it finally happened. I purchased my first house with the new company for about $30,000 in Decatur, Georgia, in 1996. I was excited and scared half to death at the same time. After all, I was the personal guarantor for the property. If the project failed, I would fail right along with it.

But it worked out: we rehabbed the property the best we knew how at the time, and we were able to sell the property for a modest profit. This experience was invaluable, along with all the other transactions since that point. At the very least, I learned what not to do the next time; I also learned how to rehab a property better. I became more in tune to the real estate market as a whole and the areas where I wanted to focus on purchasing and the areas to avoid.

But this early experience was even more invaluable than I imagined. During the process of rehabbing homes, and after going through the terrible experiences of undependable contractors, I met a gentleman to whom I was referred by a church member who owned his own construction company. The year was 1999, and he had relocated to Atlanta in 1996 to take advantage of the booming real estate market from the Olympics. He was an expert in residential construction and was looking to get a foothold in the Atlanta market in construction and investing. He helped rehab a few of my properties and even got me out of a jam or two that another contractor had left me in with a previous property. I saw that he was dependable, did quality work, and that he was in it for the long haul. As a result of this encounter, he taught me the construction business, and I taught him the real estate investing business. My passion was definitely in construction, development, and investing.

To this very day, some twenty years later, that gentleman has been my project manager and/or partner in multiple construction projects, rehabs, and new construction, both residential and commercial. Also in 1999, my first company, which was the real estate investment and mortgage company outfit, came to an end, as my focus then solely shifted to real estate investing, construction, and development.

Over the course of that twenty-year span, I have started numerous companies and have continued training and education in real estate investing, real estate sales, rehabbing, and new construction. To date, I have purchased and sold several hundred homes in the metro Atlanta area as an investor, have built multiple homes from the ground up, and have rehabbed and/or renovated millions of dollars' worth of construction projects. I have also been a franchise owner of HomeVestors of America—"We Buy Ugly Houses"—in the metro Atlanta area. My current company has served as a preferred vendor with multinational insurance companies to provide restoration services for insurance claims. I have been invited to multiple speaking engagements, participated in radio interviews, and I have provided numerous consulting services on multiple levels.

I said all of that to say this: I feel confident with the experiences that I have, including the peaks and the valleys, coupled with the tremendous highs and lows that I have experienced in this business, that I have some helpful insight and wisdom that I can share with you as it pertains to real estate investing. If I can at least shine the light, impart knowledge, and help one person in this area, then it will all have been worth it. With the knowledge and technology that are readily available in today's time, coupled with the techniques that I will share with you in this book, you can be well on your way to make REAL money in real estate investing.

CHAPTER 1

Fix 'n' Flips

HOW OFTEN HAVE we heard advertisements on the radio and TV claiming that you can buy houses with no money down and how real estate investing is so easy that even a novice can do it? Well, I don't want to rain on the parade, but I see things differently. Yes, you can make money in real estate, and you can even buy a house with no money down, but not because of the reasons that they lead us to believe. In the coming chapters, I will explain how these scenarios can become reality.

It all starts with a strategy. Real estate investing is very broad and complex, better to be approached with a laser-focus strategy as opposed to a shotgun method. What I mean by this is that I think you will save time, energy, and money by knowing your niche and what you want to accomplish before you start investing as opposed to starting and trying to figure it out along the way.

Businessdictionary.com defines a strategy as "a plan of action or policy designed to achieve a major or overall aim; master plan or grand design."

In this book, I have identified five strategies to real estate investing. In this chapter, we will focus on one of the strategies known as "fix 'n' flips." Simply put, fix 'n' flips involve purchasing a property—usually a distressed property; repairing the house—known as rehab; and the selling the property for retail value—usually done by listing the property on a multiple listing service (MLS).

Purchase the property for low, rehab it, and sell it for high at full value.

There are three of what I call *pillars*, or foundational pieces, needed in accomplishing your goal or strategy to be successful in fix 'n' flips.

Let me use a sports analogy. When a basketball team is built in today's NBA, it seems that a team needs at least three superstars in order to make it to the championship. Likewise, in real estate investing, you will need at least three superstar team members in order to be successful in fix 'n' flips. These three pillars of success are: acquisitions, financing, and contracting. Now, ultimately, it's always wise to have other good contributing team members, but you must have knowledge and be successful in the areas of acquisitions, financing, and contracting in order to be successful with fix 'n' flips.

Acquisitions is the process by which you acquire your property. You must purchase the property first before any process of rehabbing and selling can begin. What is your strategy or plan to acquire the properties?

Acquisitions is a major pillar needed to run a successful real estate investing business. To have a thorough acquisition plan that will consistently bring forth a pool of properties to choose from, you will need the following plan in place:

- Real estate agent

- Wholesalers

- Mailers/postcards

- Investor-to-investor

- Bird dogs

- Drive neighborhoods

CHAPTER 2

Real Estate Agent

YOUR *REAL ESTATE* *agent* is one superstar member that you need on your team. Choose a good real estate agent who understands real estate investing and is available and willing to work with you to grow your business. Your real estate agent superstar will help you gain access to the largest pool of potential properties in any city, and that is the MLS. At any given point, there may be tens of thousands of properties on the market for sale, and your superstar agent has access to these properties and can assist you in placing offers to purchase on many of the properties that you select.

Your agent will also have access to "comps," which are comparable sales that have taken place in the area. This is vital in determining the value of the property. Comparable sales information can be gathered for the purchase price of the distressed property on the front end as well as the full value price of what the property is worth on the back end after the repairs have been done.

Agents also have the ability to network within their office or with other agents and sellers in the area. Oftentimes, through their networking, they may be able to introduce you to a property before the general public has full knowledge of the property. The more properties that you close with your superstar agent, the more they will work for you to bring additional deals to your attention.

Keep in mind that oftentimes in this business, it's a numbers game, meaning the more offers to purchase that you submit, the more the sellers will counteroffer or accept your offer. Imagine if you submit ten offers to purchase; you may engage with three or four of the sellers, and you may get one acceptance. So, naturally, the more offers you submit, the more acceptances you will eventually get. In chapter 3, we will discuss how much to offer on each property.

Wholesalers are generally individuals or companies who have access to properties and are willing to sell you the property for a fee. Their fee is usually already included in the asking price or sales price that they present to you. They are not interested in rehabbing or holding on to the properties; they would rather wholesale the property to the professional investor and move on to the next deal. A true wholesaler has access to multiple properties, so they make their money in volume. As opposed to trying to get rich off one deal, they generally add $5,000–$10,000 profit onto the property and still sell it to you for less than the market value of the property. Most of the time, the wholesaler's properties are considered as "off market" deals because they are not listed on the MLS, so they are private deals.

Wholesalers generally have a mailing list of buyers, and once they have a property for sale, they will email their buyers' list to inform them of the property. Generally speaking, if the wholesaler is asking for a fair price, the properties will be placed under contract or flat-out purchased by buyers from the email list in a matter of days, if not hours. Therefore, you would be wise to network and become knowledgeable of the legitimate wholesalers in your area. Once you do, be sure to get their information and get added to their list of buyers so that you can receive the emails once a property becomes available.

Buyer beware! For the novice investor, please be aware that there are a lot of would-be wholesalers, fake wholesalers, and pretenders. Transactions through genuine wholesalers are usually very quick and nonrefundable. Oftentimes, they do not allow for due diligence periods, as is the case when purchasing from the MLS. These deals are quick transactions, and once you pay your earnest money deposit and/or close on the property, it's yours, even if it has defects. Be careful to do your own homework on values, cost of construction, comps in the area, and so forth, as many wholesalers will do this for you, and oftentimes, the numbers may be skewed in such a way that it benefits them more in order to sell the property. Again, this is an area that your superstar agent can help you to accurately determine values in the area and repairs needed to bring the house up to par to sell. That way you can make an informed decision on whether you should purchase the property or not and at what price.

Mailers/postcards are very helpful marketing tools that will allow you to get immediately in front of homeowners who may be willing to sell their property directly to you without putting the property on the market to the general public, also known as "off-market deals." Generally speaking, the savvy investor will select a community, a zip code, or neighborhood that they are familiar with or interested in purchasing homes. With this targeted approach, they will produce a handwritten letter or professionally designed mailer or postcard introducing themselves as a professional buyer and that they are currently purchasing properties in the area. If the homeowner is interested in selling their property, you are willing to make them an offer to purchase and to close quickly, hassle free! There are no appraisals needed and no real estate commission to pay, thereby creating a quick, inexpensive way to sell the property in its current condition, regardless of repairs needed—all of this for a discounted sell price.

In short, the mailer/postcard method should be a targeted marketing campaign that is just one piece of the pie. This should be a constant drip to the community where you are interested in buying homes so that in the event an owner is ready to sell, they will have already been introduced to your company many times over. It's been said by some marketing gurus that the average person needs to see a company name, logo, phone number, and so forth, a minimum of seven or eight times before they really recognize the brand. This is known as an "impression." Your targeted marketing campaign should be a regular message that is getting out to the community maybe once or twice a month. Keep in mind that the purchase and sale of one house could more than pay for the marketing cost for months on end.

Investor-to-investor is a good way to network and get introduced to new properties for sale. Oftentimes, your peers may have properties or access to properties that they may not be able to purchase or finance the repairs at that time and would be willing to transfer the deal to you for a fee. Many times, your peers may already have the property under contract and can "assign the contract" to you. Assigning the contract is a legal method of transferring the contract that another entity has to you to purchase as long as you uphold the terms and conditions of the existing contract from the first entity. You can find many investor-to-investor opportunities at your local real estate investors' organization, through social media, and through national and local investor seminars.

A *bird dog* is a real estate investor term generally referring to an individual who finds real estate deals and brings them to you. Usually this person is new to the business or is trying to learn the real estate business in a method similar to on-the-job training. Most of the time, this person does not have the capital to purchase the property themselves; as a result, they will bring the deal to you for a referral fee or commission, typically between $500 to $2,500 per deal, upon closing. Oftentimes, bird dogs rely on relatives, friends, or neighbors who live in the same community that they do who may be aware of someone looking to sell their property quickly, and generally in as-is condition without doing any repairs.

Bird dogs can be helpful, especially in their own communities. It is conceivable that you could have multiple bird dogs working for you, bringing deals from time to time. Also, some college students or recent graduates looking to make extra money on the side can make good bird dogs. They can drive particular communities and make note of vacant houses or houses for sale by owner, talk to neighbors, and even attend neighborhood meetings or functions to gain more knowledge of the area.

Drive neighborhoods. Sometimes nothing beats good old-fashioned driving. We used to say that there is gold in driving the neighborhoods. Plain and simple, if you drive the areas long enough, you will see signs with properties for sale that you may not have seen in the MLS, you will meet neighbors, and you will become more acquainted with what the neighborhood trends and home values are. Good things happen when you drive the neighborhoods where you want to be. You even get a better perspective of home remodels, color schemes, various renovation nuances in the area and, equally as important, what your competition is doing in the market. A wise investor sets aside time each week or every other week to intentionally drive the neighborhoods to stay abreast of what's happening in the area.

CHAPTER 3

Financing

FINANCING IS ANOTHER major pillar needed to have a successful real estate investing business. Having the ability to structure and finance the purchase of your properties in a timely manner is a critical component to real estate investing. That is why your _lender_ is the second superstar team member whom I have identified to go along with your superstar agent. The various forms of financing that can help you in your investing business include:

- Hard money lenders

- Private lenders

- Cash

Hard money lenders came on the scene probably in the early to mid-'90s. They filled a void left by traditional banks/lenders as it pertains to real estate investing. The banks viewed real estate investing as risky and speculative, which it probably is, but there is no doubt that this marketplace has arrived—and in a big way. I don't see this market going away anytime soon. But traditionally speaking, banks were not lending money on speculative real estate. Therefore, hard money lenders stepped into the void and provided real estate investors the financing that they needed to purchase and rehab this speculative real estate, and once rehabbed to full value, it was no longer speculative—it was a market value piece of real estate.

However, there was a caveat for the lenders taking on this risk. The lenders were operating in a new space, a space in which they were not regulated by the SEC, FDIC, or any of the governing bodies that regulate traditional banks. As a result, the lenders charged whatever amount of money in interest and fees that they could get away with. Some of the early numbers were 15–18 percent interest rates and five to six points in fees paid to the lender at closing. These were standard numbers well into the early 2000s.

Now, there are a number of hard money lenders in the marketplace; therefore, it has created more competition, and now the interest and fees have gone down considerably from where they used to be. Still, hard money lenders serve a purpose, which is the ability to purchase and rehab a property with one loan so it can become a full market value property worth twice as much as it did when purchased. And teaming up with the right lender can help you to grow your business tremendously.

Today's hard money lenders are usually small finance companies that specialize in the real estate investment market. They have knowl-edge of the city and surrounding communities in terms of property values, and they are accustomed to lending to new and experienced investors in this market space. They generally have a relationship with a closing attorney and local appraiser who serves as appraiser and inspector to make sure that the money that has been borrowed to repair the houses actually gets applied for that purpose. The hard money lenders generally have a presence and market to everywhere the local investors are, be it investor associations, seminars, online, word of mouth, and so forth.

I need to caution you again: not all hard money lenders are the same. Please do your research on the local hard money lenders and choose the ones with a good reputation. There are some hard money lenders who are in the business of acquiring the investors' properties that they lend on as soon as the investor makes a mistake or is delin-quent on their payments. Please keep in mind that it depends on the state. Georgia is a "nonjudicial foreclosure state," meaning these lend-ers have the right to foreclose on your property without filing suit or appearing in court before a judge. Simply put, it can be worded in the closing documents you sign that if you are late in making payments, the lender does not have to accept your late payment—they can immediately move forward with foreclosing because their interest was in the property from the very beginning and not lending you the money.

Private lenders, or private money lenders (PMLs), seem to be the trend now. Over recent years, PMLs have emerged onto the scene and appear to be a preferred method of financing. PMLs are usually high-net-worth individuals, family members, or friends who will finance you or, better yet, invest in you as the borrower with the expectation of getting a certain percentage return on their investment (ROI).

Typically, it works like this: most lenders will lend to a borrower purchasing an investment property an amount equal to or less than 70 percent of the after-repair value of the property. If a property is worth $100,000 after all repairs are done and it is in tip-top shape, a lender will lend up to $70,000 up front, but this amount must include the purchase and repair amount. In addition, they usually want to see the borrower/buyer have skin in the game by coming to the table with at least 10–15 percent down.

In this scenario, the lender may lend $60,000 and expect the borrower to bring a $10,000 down payment. This is when the private money lender kicks in. The PML could provide the $10,000 down payment or gap financing that the borrower needs if the borrower doesn't have it. Especially if the purchase price of the house and the repairs are much higher than this scenario, the 10 percent down payment amount could be significantly higher, and having that PML partner is crucial in being able to close the deal. Most PML expect about a 20 percent return on their money. In other words, if they invest $10,000 into the deal, it is understood that they will receive their $10,000 back plus $2,000 in interest upon closing of the property. Most closing attorneys can draft the legal paperwork to ensure that the PML gets paid off the top upon selling the house.

Please don't underestimate the value of having one or multiple PML partners. These individuals often have full-time jobs in unrelated fields but have the funds and are willing to invest in you and your project for the next six months to get a return on their money as opposed to leaving it in the stock market. These funds are usually discretionary funds or easily accessible funds that can be gathered quickly in time for closing.

Cash is always king in the real estate investing business. Remember, financing is a major pillar in running a successful business, so if you are fortunate enough to be in a position where you have cash and are not in need of financing, then you are ahead of the game. Oftentimes, sellers are willing to sell to buyers at a significant discount in exchange for a quick cash closing. Some cash investors will even use a combination of financing and their own cash to eliminate the need for PML and to acquire more projects at a time.

CHAPTER 4

Contracting

THE THIRD MAJOR pillar of success needed in the real estate investing business is *contracting*. Your construction contractor can make or break your whole deal. So much is riding on the back of the contractor that oftentimes, we lose sight of just how valuable this team member is. That is why your *contractor* is the other super star team member.

I admit that as a licensed general contractor in Georgia for many years, I may be a little biased, but having a reputable, dependable contractor partner on the team can elevate your business to the next level. Sure, contractors get a bad rap, like used car salespeople, and there are many crappy would-be contractors, but you must weed them out and team up with a reputable professional contractor. Think of it this way: all of the work that is done up front during the due diligence process to determine cost of repairs, after-repair values, and so forth, depends upon the contractor doing his or her job and rehabbing the property to a level that will increase the value of the property as anticipated. Bad rehab means bad values; good rehab means great values.

As a contractor, I take pride in the work that I do. I treat every property as if it were my own. I would not put anything into a house that I wouldn't put into my own unless, of course, it is an absolute request of the owner. Keep in mind that good help can be hard to find, especially in the construction business; therefore, your contractor has the job of not only finding and maintaining quality, skilled workers but also managing the sequence and order of construction, managing the timeframe to complete the project, and of course, managing the budget agreed upon to get the work done.

For those of you who are not familiar with contractors or the construction space as it pertains to rehabbing, you will need to become somewhat knowledgeable if you want to participate in fix 'n' flip properties as an investment strategy. Plumbers, electricians, carpenters, and so forth are all tradespeople. They specialize in a trade and are experts in that particular discipline. However, in order to complete the renovation of a house, it will generally require multiple tradespeople, such as drywallers, flooring installers, painters, and so forth, in addition to the plumbers and electricians just mentioned. Therefore, a general contractor may be needed to manage and/or oversee the operation of each tradesperson or company to make sure that all disciplines are professionally and successfully done so that the newly renovated property is up to code, is repaired to high quality, and will ultimately increase and maintain the value of the renovated home. A general contractor is oftentimes an individual or a company that is responsible for the day-to-day oversight of the project, management of the vendors and tradespeople, and the communication of all pertinent information between the property owner and other stakeholders throughout the construction process. Your contractor is a vital piece of the process in helping to turn a distressed, underperforming property into a thriving, appreciating asset that is tangible.

There are a lot of contractors out there in every city. I recommend that you hire or team up with licensed contractors who can warranty their work, who are stable and have been in business for a while, and who have the financial wherewithal to take responsibility in case of corrections or adjustments that may be needed. You can find these contractors by word of mouth, visits to current jobsites, or lists from local licensing boards or reputable associations.

CHAPTER 5

Buy and Hold

BUY AND HOLD is an investment strategy usually done by the more experienced investor or the investor who has laser focus on building a rental portfolio. Obviously, rental properties can be a tremendous platform to build wealth through the increased values of the properties over the years as well as by the potential monthly residual rental income.

Oftentimes investors will use a three-to-one ratio when building a rental portfolio. Simply put, for every three fix 'n' flip properties that are purchased, rehabbed, and then sold, investors will rehab and keep one property as a rental. Therefore, they realize the lump sum cash from the sale of three properties before they hold on to the one that generally does not produce an initial lump sum payout once the repairs have been completed.

Some investors have determined that every property that they can get their hands on will be a rental. For these individuals, they obviously either have a plan, or they are in a financial position in which they are not in need of cashing out on each property and would rather build the portfolio long term and realize their gains that way.

There is another option with some lenders. Some lenders have a rental program loan product that would allow investors to refinance out of their hard money short-term financing into a permanent long-term loan designed for rentals. Using the $100,000 after-repair value scenario in chapter 3 (in which the borrower was in the property at no more than $70,000, which included a $10,000 down payment), this new rental program loan product would allow the investors to refinance at

80 percent loan to value (LTV), which is $80,000. This allows the short-term loan of $70,000 to be paid off, and they can pocket $10,000 and keep the property, now with an $80,000 long-term loan with a 7–8 percent interest rate, which can be used as a rental.

Airbnb properties is also another strategy that investors use to generate monthly income and/or to build their rental portfolio. Airbnb is an online marketplace that connects people who want to rent their homes with people who are looking for accommodations in that city or location. Oftentimes, investors will buy properties, rehab them, and place them on the Airbnb marketplace strictly to rent the homes on an ongoing basis. The Airbnb phenomenon came on the scene a few years ago, and it has a list of pros and cons to be taken under consideration before you decide to invest in this strategy.

Some of the pros include its ability to provide monthly residual income. Depending on the location of the property and how well the host maintains its upkeep and cleanliness, as an Airbnb home, there is a real chance that the property can generate a consistent monthly income from individuals wanting to rent the property for short-term or long-term stays. Many times, if the property remains rented for most of the month, it can generate more money per month than a tenant with a fixed monthly rate because Airbnb homes generally rent for more on a daily rate than a fixed tenant rate.

The cons are somewhat obvious in terms of more people coming in and out of the home than a full-time tenant, which may increase the odds of hosting the less-than-desirable renter who may not maintain the property as well. Also, you would need a dependable cleaning crew who can come back and forth to the property on a regular basis to have the house cleaned and prepared for the next guest.

CHAPTER 6

Buy and Build

BUY AND BUILD is one of my favorite strategies mainly because I am passionate about new construction projects. I have built a number of homes from the ground up in the metro Atlanta area. This strategy can be employed in the form of in-field building in which the investors purchase individual developed lots usually found in town or in existing subdivisions, or tract building in which the investor/builder purchases a tract of land and develops the land and builds the houses.

One of the joys that I have experienced as a builder is being able to drive down a street and see a house that I built from the ground up and know that now it is a home and safe haven for some deserving family. It makes me recall seeing the vacant lot with nothing on it except maybe overgrown trees or grass. Then, with the team of architects and other design professionals, we all create a vision of taking nothing and building a structure on it that will last for generations to come. It's one of the great joys of the business.

This strategy can be very profitable as well. New construction houses typically fare well on the market once they are built and ready to sell. The key with new construction is what you do on the front end. You make your money based upon where and how you buy the land. Remember, location, location, location is key but also price, price, price. The rule of thumb in building is your lot price should not be more than 20 percent of the after-repair value. In other words, just using roundabout figures, if the house will be worth $250,000 after construction, you should not pay more than $50,000 for the lot. The purchase of the lot should be no more than 20 percent of the value of the house upon completion.

Many metro areas have individual lots that were not built out when the other existing houses were built. Some lots are just completely covered with trees, some lots had houses or structures on them years ago but were demolished, and on some lots, the original builder just did not finish the development. Whatever the reason, the land is vacant. For the investor/builder using the buy and build strategy, the investor will locate these vacant lots and will calculate the cost to build a new house on it that will blend in with the existing architecture in the area as well as the up-and-coming price point. In today's time, we are seeing a resurgence of property values in the downtown markets, as many homebuyers are interested in living in the downtown areas closer to parks, amenities, jobs, and entertainment areas. As a result, the investors are realizing tremendous gains on the back end after the house or townhome is built, provided that the purchase of the land was within the formula.

Tract builders have identified smaller tracts of land that have never been developed. This land can either be in town or just on the outskirts. For the builders who have found land in town and are knowledgeable or skilled enough to develop the tract—which means bringing in the infrastructure, sewer, streets, curbing, and so forth—they usually build smaller, intimate communities, often townhome-style communities, and are able to establish a new market value price. This can be extremely profitable because the builder/developer is actually creating something that never existed; therefore, they are setting the market for the price of each unit. This type of development is reserved for the experienced builder with the financial position to withstand a one- to two-year project but will undoubtedly be rewarded handsomely upon completion of the community.

CHAPTER 7

Multifamily

MULTIFAMILY PROPERTIES ARE basically residential housing with two or more units under one roof or several buildings within a complex. Multifamily housing can accommodate multiple tenants, each having its own living area to include kitchen, bedrooms, and bathrooms. When we refer to multifamily housing, we are speaking of housing units anywhere from duplexes to condos to very large apartment buildings. Investing in multifamily projects is a tremendous way to build wealth in your real estate portfolio. Not only do you accumulate equity from the building itself, but you also enjoy income from multiple renters each month.

Generally speaking, multifamily projects are often taken on by the experienced investor or the investor who has the financial wherewithal to put the hefty down payment into the project that most lenders require. For lenders who are in this space, most will lend about 75 percent of the purchase price of the building. Therefore, the investor will be responsible for about a 25 percent buy-in, or skin in the game. Many investors opt for multifamily projects in which the buildings are already leased with at least a two-to-three-year track record. Oftentimes, the property will already have a management company in place that is familiar with the process of collecting rent, performing maintenance and upkeep of the buildings, and managing the overall profit and expense of the property.

In my opinion, the rental market will continue to increase in most in-town areas as the price of housing and the challenges of buying a new home increase. Many tenants will opt to just rent a house, condo, or apartment. As a result, the savvy investor who owns these multi-family properties stands to realize tremendous gains by providing quality rentals in desirable areas. This market can be very competitive, as most profitable real estate markets are; therefore, having a skilled real estate agent is recommended to not only locate these hidden gems but to also assist with making sure the right team is in place for the management and upkeep of these properties.

The successful multifamily investor stands to boost his or her portfolio with consistent monthly cash flow, all while enjoying long-term gains while the equity in the building continues to grow. Therefore, as a real estate investing strategy, multifamily investing is high on the list.

In addition, many investors opt to start small with duplexes and/or triplexes first and then work their way up to larger apartment buildings. There should be existing inventory of duplexes and triplexes for sale on the MLS at any given time in most cities. There is also another website that focuses on multifamily buildings (www.loopnet.com). If you enter the city where you are interested in purchasing, it will provide a listing of several commercial and multifamily buildings for sale. Some listings will come with a turnkey system in place, such as a management company, which will be familiar with the property and have all of the rental history and property upkeep data easily accessible, while other listings may be just distressed properties with no current tenants. In this case, the savvy investor will have the opportunity to purchase a below value property and utilize the buy and hold technique to rehab the property to increase the property value and rental readiness, refinance out of the short-term acquisition loan into a more permanent long-term loan, and ensure that the rental amount coming in from the multiple units will more than cover the mortgage and upkeep expenses, to allow for a monthly profit.

CHAPTER 8

Tax Liens

A PROPERTY TAX lien is a legal claim against a property for unpaid property taxes. A tax lien may be imposed for delinquent taxes owed on real property or personal property, or as a result of failure to pay income taxes or other taxes. A tax lien prohibits a property from being sold or refinanced until the taxes are paid and the lien is removed.

For the professional investor, having the knowledge and expertise in the field of tax lien investing can be a very lucrative real estate investing strategy. In the state of Georgia, property taxes are generally due in September or October each year. As a result, each year when the taxes become due, hundreds, if not thousands, of properties become delinquent in taxes owed to the county for various reasons such as out-of-state owners, vacant houses, sick or incapacitated owners, owners not being aware of their tax bills, and the like. This results in a huge amount of money being owed to the county tax commissioner that has not been collected.

Some properties have years of property taxes owed to the county. Eventually, the tax office will place a tax lien, also known as a FIFA, on the property for years of delinquent taxes. Oftentimes, large finance companies that are in the business of tax lien investing will have a prearranged agreement with the tax commissioner. The arrangement essentially allows the finance company to come in and purchase delinquent taxes, or FIFAs, for hundreds or even thousands of properties that have been issued tax liens by the tax office. This is in exchange for a huge check the finance company will write the tax commissioner to help them collect their tax money immediately while the finance company now has a stake or partial ownership in said properties, all with the stroke of a pen. So it really is a win-win situation for the county tax office and the finance company because they both get what they want; however, it is not so much for the property owner.

So you may have asked the question: Why does a finance company want to buy delinquent real estate taxes? A fair question. The catch is this: when an investor, such as the finance company or any other investor, purchases the unpaid taxes from the tax office, the property owner now owes the investor the same amount of money owed for the delinquent taxes plus a 20 percent fee or markup. The property owner now has twelve months to redeem or pay off the new investor, as the property owner no longer owes the county tax commissioner because the finance company paid them up front. The owner now owes the finance company or investor. If this money is not paid within the twelve-month period, the investor can now file for a procedure similar to a foreclosure, known as "quiet title," which literally wipes the property free and clear from all liens and encumbrances, and the ownership of the property will now belong to the investor, as the property owner has lost their property due to failure to pay delinquent property taxes.

The finance company is in it for the 20 percent finance fee. Just imagine a huge company dropping millions of dollars on the table to purchase thousands of tax FIFAs with a guaranteed 20 percent return on the majority of the properties, and with the ones that don't pay, they end up confiscating the property and selling it for more in the marketplace! That is really the essence of tax lien investing.

Seasoned investors have taken this concept and are implementing it on a smaller scale. They may purchase one or two tax FIFAs at a time, with the hopes of ending up with either 20 percent return on the money or the property itself.

I am reminded of a time when I wanted to enter into this marketplace. I actually purchased a tax lien from the finance company. At that point, I now owned the rights to the property, and the property owner owed me the cost of the delinquent taxes plus 20 percent. When I finally got in touch with the property owner and I went out to the property to explain that they owed the tax payment to me or they could lose the house, I discovered an elderly single lady who had lived in the house for years and was totally unaware that taxes were owed on the property—nor did she have the financial ability to pay for it. This scenario played in my mind over and over again, and for me, morally, I couldn't move forward. I was fortunate enough to go back to the finance company and reverse the transaction because I was not willing to continue with that process. I was able to explain that to the homeowner, and my hope was that she was able to at least get on a payment plan with the finance company. That was the only time that I purchased a tax lien. Please keep in mind that all transactions are different and that oftentimes, the property could be vacant, so this can still be a viable investment strategy.

Conclusion

IN CLOSING, *Find It, Fix It, Flip It* is a how-to guide filled with information, instructions, and nuggets on how to develop strategies in an effort to be successful in the real estate investing arena. Real estate is such a broad and competitive field that oftentimes, newer investors need help to navigate this process. Just knowing the dos and don'ts and getting firsthand impartation on ideas and strategies can be the difference between a profitable project or even a successful, lasting career in this field. Remember, the five investment strategies are fix 'n' flips, buy and hold, buy and build, multifamily, and tax liens. The three pillars or cornerstones of investing are acquisitions, financing, and contracting. Finally, the three superstar team members are real estate agent, lender, and contractor. It is better to be laser focused than to have a shotgun approach.

My goal has been to shed light and to shed wisdom based upon years of experience and trials and errors in this business. If information from these pages can help many people or even just one person, then it will have been all worth it for me. Each one, teach one!

I have enjoyed the challenge of putting this book together over the weeks and months that it took, and I hope that it has been an easy read but also inspirational and informative. Now it's up to you to take action.

A goal is only a dream until you write it down!
—Emmitt Smith

I wish you much success in all of your endeavors to find meaning and purpose in your life and career. Always remember that success is relative. Each person has a different definition and meaning of what is considered success. To me, even reading this book with the hopes and desire to learn something new and to better oneself is a progressive and successful mindset. See it on the inside first, and no doubt the universe will bring it to you where you see it manifested in your life. You are fearfully and wonderfully made, created with a purpose that only you can do!

Please share any updates and testimonials with me.
Godspeed!

Scott H. Williams
scott@gatewayconstrutionco.com

Acknowledgements

I HAVE OFTEN wondered what it would be like to receive an award and to thank all the people who believed in you and made it possible to be in that moment. Well, this is my opportunity to do so. This is the part where I get a little emotional because working twenty-five years as an entrepreneur is difficult, regardless of the industry. There is a story to tell, and mine is no different.

First and above all things, I must give Glory to God! He has been my anchor in a time of storm. Words can not properly express how God has brought me such a mighty long way, and because I am assured he knows my heart, I will simply say "Thank you!"

Secondly, I am truly blessed to be surrounded by family and friends who love me and support my every move. I am humbled and truly thankful for the encouragement, the prayers, the emotional support, the financial support, the listening ear, the "whatever I need at the time that I need it" that helped me to keep going. Words will never describe what your impartation did for me through this journey. I thank you!

I would also like to thank my company team members, workers, subcontractors, and partners who were all instrumental in producing successful projects. Without this team, we would not be able to flip houses. Your expertise, your diligence, your patience with me, and your craftsmanship have all played a vital role in the success of each project and getting us to this point today. I thank you!

Last, but definitely not least, there were individuals who believed in me enough that they invested money into the real estate investing system that we created. Without these financial dollars and partnerships, none of this would be possible. Your trust in me, proven and backed by your hard-earned dollars, was a seed planted in good ground; had you not done it, none of this would be possible. I am eternally grateful to my investor team. I hope that we all will continue to grow together and produce even more successful projects in the future. Many thanks to B. Horton, C. J. Barren, B. Jackson, R. Crawford, J. Hefner, S. Hamlette, A. Angelone, M. Howse, S. Walker, D. Harris, C. Walker, and D. Henry!

Special thanks to my pastor, Creflo A. Dollar Jr. Thank you for the years of shepherding me and for being my spiritual father. Thank you for providing a safe haven and covering where I can freely worship and grow in the knowledge of God.

www.ingramcontent.com/pod-product-compliance
Lightning Source LLC
Chambersburg PA
CBHW060947130726
48001CB00003B/1098